Enoch Conklin

Conklin's modern Nineveh and Babylon

Enoch Conklin

Conklin's modern Nineveh and Babylon

ISBN/EAN: 9783337235222

Printed in Europe, USA, Canada, Australia, Japan

Cover: Foto ©Andreas Hilbeck / pixelio.de

More available books at **www.hansebooks.com**

NINEVEH AND BABYLON.

BEING A DESCRIPTION OF THE

ANCIENT PUEBLO PEOPLE,

AND THEIR DWELLINGS.

ALONG THE LINE OF THE

ATCHISON, TOPEKA & SANTA FÉ RAILROAD

AND THE

SOUTHERN PACIFIC RAILROAD OF ARIZONA,

TO

CALIFORNIA.

THE PUEBLO INDIAN.

ONE of the greatest labors of the historical and eth-
nological department of our government, is the study of
the origination and relative position of the so-called Indians of New Mexico and Arizona known as the Pueblos.
So different are they from what we generally understand
by the word "Indian" the question comes up, are they
Indian? They have never been known as a people to
lift a hand against the whites, and evidence a strong in-
clination to all pursuits of industry. They are Indians
only so far as all native inhabitants of a country are
Indians.

The Pueblo Indians are, unquestionably, descendants
of the Aztecs, of whom, after the so-called anihilation of
that people by Cortez in 1620, perhaps naught but a
single man and woman may have escaped to some hole
in the rocks or mountains and there, by the cunning
and interesting repetition of history, the beautiful story
of Adam and the Garden of Eden told over again. One
must doubt however, that these people had the nice big
red apple Eve had, by the poor specimen of that fruit
which that section of country produces. Perhaps it was
a *pinon* in this case, as this nut is the national fruit
there. It permeates every crack and corner of every
Pueblo's residence, and the little Indian girls will in-
terest you by coming upon the train when it reaches
Isletta, and vending their dried and shrivelled up apples,

and their sweet *Pinons*. A prolific year of the *pinon* indicates pestilence, and makes them a "forbidden fruit" in those seasons. The girls come in their native costumes, and sing out in their musical voices their "*Cari Pinons*." In these girls one can see a Pocahontas, and find many an American who, like Wm. Penn, fell a willing captive to their simple charms. It is estimated there are about one hundred Anglo-Saxon whites married, legally and in the solemnization of all religious sects, to Pueblo Indian girls in New Mexico; raising families, and thus raising the standard of civilization in the Pueblo of their adopted parentage.

No one going to California by the Southern or "Sunset" route, should fail to visit some of the native Pueblo towns and their people. One of the most formidable and accessible of these is La Guna. Leaving the main line of the Santa Fé Road at Albuquerque, you go out on the Atlantic & Pacific Railroad only sixty miles. The train runs around the foot of the hill on which the town is built. The hill might be called a small mountain or plateau. *La Guna* interpreted means "The Water." This is evidently given because a stream circuits the mount, on its course to the valley below; and water, in that section of country is most thoroughly appreciated by those there. Here the ancient building of Egypt and their people, Nubian in character, may be seen carrying water in jars upon their heads, like the descendants of Rebecca of Bible fame. As one approaches this ancient cluster, and if he has ever traveled the Holy Land, the exclamation "Joppa from the North," or "Babylon" is apt to escape his lips, and he seems to have discovered remnants of Bible History in our own land.

ALTHOUGH not existing wholly in Arizona, the
proximity of the Zuni and Moqui villages and its
people, the Territory together with its associate inter-
ests, prevent us from passing this wonderful people
unnoticed.

The old tribe of the Zuni inhabit a region extending on both sides of the line between Arizona and
New Mexico. They are destined to prove, or, perhaps,
are the most interesting of all our aborigines, probably
on account of our ignorance of them. The habitation
of these people comprise seven cities—three of which
are known as the Moqui villages, and are in Arizona.
The main *Pueblo* or village is situated in the fertile
and picturesque Zuni valley.

The first and leading feature in a visit to this people
is their village, or the system under which they exist
as a community. The whole tribe of the Zuni, which

in '76, numbered about three thousand people, live in one settlement. Their houses are not detached as in ordinary cities, but are a system of houses massed together in one grand structure, in the following manner. An elevated section of country which overlooks the surrounding lowlands and valleys, is selected. A position on this elevation, where portions of it gives a slope of perhaps 45° or more, is also chosen. Up this incline, the houses, or the sections of the one grand house, are built—the one over-lapping the previous one to about a quarter or a third of its area. The one in the Zuni valley is six stories high, commencing at the first house, or at the bottom of the hill, you approach by a ladder, to the top of that house, and there you find the entrance (or the front door) of that house, in the place where the skylight of an American house is situated. From the roof of this house you approach the same way, by the ladder, the top of the succeeding house, or section of the great house, and proceed to enter it as you did the previous one. So this system is carried on throughout this communal condition of life. The size of the whole may be comprehended when we say it covers twelve acres. The second leading feature is the type of some of the subjects. A few have nearly white hair, resembling generally what is termed an English tow-head. It is only occasionally you will see one; and whether these are a

A NAVAJO INDIAN BOY.

phenomena in the one race, or a remnant of another, is as yet, a query to the ethnologist. Also, specimens will be found exhibiting pink or blue eyes. Both of these classes are however, rare. In the absence of any method of chronicling events being found among them, they afford ample scope for the culture of the historian. Where they came from is as anxious an inquiry of the ethnologist as the question "Where are they destined to go to?" is with the psychologist or religionist. It is supposed that the style of dwellings is the result of necessary protection of by-gone times. Whether Cortes and his allies; whether more subsequently, the treacherous Mexican desperado of which at no distant day this country, was infested, perhaps either of these could best tell us, or whether the unmerciful persecutions of a more formidable tribe of Indians, is a question perhaps the ancestors of the warlike Apachè of Arizona could answer. I am of the opinion it was some condition of the latter. All the region of country included within the limits of New Mexico and Arizona already traveled over or explored, brings to the surface new evidences of persecution, annihilation or submission.

One body of ruins covering an area of many acres on the east side of the Colorado, between Yuma (Arizona City) and Ehrenberg, exhibit one of these interesting sections, where nothing remains to trace the origin, duration or occupation. Whether it was an extensive camp of permanent miners who were murdered by Indians, or ransacked or annihilated by outlaws, is likely to remain a secret. In the absence of positive knowledge we are apt to concede it to the rapacity of the more fierce and warlike Apachés.

Although void of any system of chronicling events, like all the Indians of our West, the Zuni are in all other respects far superior, from the Anglo-Saxon stand-point of civilization. They are thrifty and frugal. Their lands extend for a distance of ten miles east and west of the boundary line between Arizona and New Mexico, and seem to have been chosen with good discretion as they embody some of the finest agricultural lands on this region. For the distance of upwards of a hundred miles south of the Zuni village there is an arroya embracing a series of small valleys, watered by mountain streams and a system of natural springs which, could the device of man cause to share their lot with the otherwise fertile soil of the so-called deserts of the western part of the State, would cause that emblematic desert rose to assume all its brilliancy. The little valley of the Zuni is about six miles wide at the longitude of the Zuni village, and runs jnst here, almost due east and west. The Zuni village is located on the north side of the Zuni river, which runs directly through the centre of the valley. The valley is dotted here and there with mesas, on one of which the Zuni villages are built; and from the elevation of which, ranging from twenty-five to a hundred feet, a most charming view may be obtained for three miles each way across the valley. It reminds one somewhat of the cheerful views in many of the upland valleys of Mexico. Valleys, hills and dales, nooks, rocks, and the like, present here that necessary diversity that pleases the sight, and which characterizes the Territory of Arizona as the traveler goes eastward.

The crops of these people are raised without irrigation. Their principal products are corn, wheat, barley, pumpkins, melons, beans, and most of the vegetables; and in importance and quantity range in about the order given—corn being the largest crop. Over the mesas and in the beautiful valleys may be seen handsomely arranged garden spots equal in neatness and attractiveness to those of the Teutons. Peach orchards varying from a quarter of an acre down. Red pepper, garlic and the smaller vegetables are raised in gardens of various dimensions, and the gardens are symbols of symmetrical neatness and cleanness. They are attended and cultivated by the women and children. Although in this respect, they would seem to resemble the Indians in custom; but from the fact that the men give their energies and time to the field products, they would seem to be a medium be-tween the aborigines and anglo-saxon element. They reminded me in this respect very much of the German. The gardens do better with some little irrigation, and the women and children do this by carrying water in vessels resembling the Mexican olla, placed on their heads. The ollas are of all sizes, and hold anywhere from one quart to ten gallons. The wells are of an original plan. They have no windlass or a means of a "drop." The ground is first dug until water is reached. An incline is then dug down to the bottom of the well, from a point sufficiently distant from the mouth of the well, to give it an angle for easy walking, digging out all the earth, and leaving a complete road-way to the bottom of the well or spring at the lower end of the hill. One of these wells I saw, measured forty feet deep and twelve square and had an incline approach of one hundred feet. It is an odd and pleas-ing sight to watch these "Rebeccas" trotting down to the well with their vessels on their head, and from their neat appearancé and docile manners one has a profound respect and an exalted opinion of Indian life, after having come from the land of the greasy "Dig-ger" or the rapacious A'paché. In their gardens one will scarcely find a weed.

In the morning the men may be seen going in files to their fields—that is, provided you "turn out" at five

in the morning. The division of work and rest for the day is very similar to the most semi-tropical countries. They go to the fields at early dawn, return to breakfast at ten o'clock (having taken a small morsel of something before going out, the same as they do in the West Indies). They do no work again until about three in the afternoon, avoiding the broiling sun, then they return to the field at that time and work until sun-down.

The country being a pastoral one to a very large extent, much stock is raised. The principal of which is sheep. On one occasion in 1872, one of the Caziques made his daughter a present of three thousand head of sheep.

Goats, cattle, horses, mules, burros, (a species of the jackass) hogs, chickens etc., form no small part of their possessions. These people are very domestic. The men do not gamble nor become as a rule, intoxicated; a condition that has become almost identical with the most of American Indians.

The chastity of the women is proverbial, and the morality of the men is beyond reproach. In the Zuni villages, women are as fair as alabaster, and as pure as virgin marble. Even to this very day it cannot but be gleaned, by an association with them, that any one who would tamper with their sacred virtue would meet with the fate of the famous guide, Estervan, who suffered death for having secretly made love to their women.

Their pastimes consist in music and dancing, and games, the chief of which is that known among them as *paleto*. It is curious to see them exert themselves at this game. It is the national game. One might sit for some time and watch them, and then have a longing to join them in their skip, hop and a jump. It is performed after this fashion :—

A line of men and boys are formed, in their bare feet. Any number may join in the game. The head one takes a stick (the *Paleto*) between his big and second toe. With this he starts off, giving two hops and a jump, at each jump, allowing his right foot to touch the ground, giving him a powerful spring. All the rest are now following close behind. Their course is round a common circle. If the *paleto* man drops his stick, the next, without stopping, picks it up with his toes, placing it in the same position as the other between his big toe and the next. If he misses, he drops out of the line while the next Indian behind tries his luck. If he picks it up he continues on until he drops it and then he drops behind to the rear, as the one who previously had done. And so they keep up, he only dropping out of the line who fails to pick up the stick when the leader has dropped it. Thus it keeps up until all but one has failed to pick up the *paleto* when dropped, and he is claimed the victor. This is witnessed by a large gathering of the women, who, clap or shout at any great alacrity of the performers, and the last one is hailed as a sort of King o' the day; has a wreath placed upon his head, and is the recipient of honors, and of presents occasionally.

This game is performed on a larger scale on fétes or holidays, and is a source of great merriment. Many a maiden will watch her lover with the most selfish anxiety for his success, and many such lovers will " lose the *paleto*" from the simple fact that the maiden is watching him. On féte days these games or performances generally end in grand processions. They have many féte days in which many historical events are commemorated. On the evenings of these days a sort of religious feast or entertainment is usually held. It is performed with great pomp and reverence. A performance which was enacted with grand ceremony attracted our attention. Some animal, usually a quadruped of some kind, this time a rabbit, was placed on the ground with his head toward the east. In its fore-paws, which are stretched out before him, is placed an ear of corn. Before this, the spirit man takes his position with a bowl of meal and with language and gestures the stranger does not understand' consecrates this meal. This being done, the animal and the ear of corn are sprinkled thoroughly with it, and a solemn exercise of prayer and consecration is gone through with. After this the animal is allowed to remain one day, and then taken up and eaten as a consecrated feast of thanksgiving for an abundant harvest. On these occasions no Mexican is allowed to enter their domain and see their processions.

The men and women alike, pet, idolize—fairly "worship" their children. Their abodes are superior —in fact, cannot be compared with what we understand as Indian huts. In style and material they resemble Mexican buildings except their houses are built as we have described, *en masse*, communial— one and each supporting the other. The principal room where the members of the tribes receive friendly visitors, are on an average nine feet high, with seats running around the structure generally covered with some unshorn skin of an animal such as a goat, sheep, wild cat, etc., making it preferable to a hard board for the sitter. The floors are of stone, and the rooms are as a general thing, neatly whitewashed; which is more than we can say of the average Mexican residences met with in Arizona. They are clean and neat always. One singular thing exists. No vermin are to be found in the whole town; neither rats, mice, roaches nor bed-bugs. A species of head lice is the only thing in that line, that ruffles their temper or destroys the equilibrium of their nerves. They are

MI-SHONG-I-NI-VI. — A VILLAGE OF THE MOQUIS IN
NORTH-EASTERN PART OF ARIZONA.

keen in trade—never getting excited or in a hurry, and "drive a bargain" with all the shrewdness of a Chatham Streeter. With an anglo-saxon training, these people, I should judge, would become one of the greatest *policy* people in the world. The spirit is innate in them; for, until the break of friendship between you and them is made flagrant, no outward manifestation is made of any slight antipathy that may exist between you upon slight provocations, that could be detected by an outside observer. The same hospitality, provided you are admitted within their limits at all, is extended to all : another evidence where the brain power has control of, and keeps the sentiments and impetuosities at bay. Let your visit be at any hour of the day or night they welcome you with this spirit. If in the night even, the same invitation for you to partake of refreshments, or to drink some of their beverages, is extended.

———

THE dress is of a cotton tunic, with a loose girdle,
extending to the knees. In cold weather a blanket, made more generally by the Moqui tribes, is
worn. Some of these blankets are of the richest designs, and will last a life time. They are mottled with
all colors and devices, and resemble, and would make
very fashionable and serviceable lap-robes as used in
American metropolitan life. Some travelers have been
known to pay as high as one hundred dollars for one
of these blankets, and it is estimated that to some of
them a whole life time has been devoted. Col. R. J.
Hinton has one of these blankets or shawls for which I
think he said he paid forty dollars, but for which he
would not take one hundred dollars cash. It puzzled
the whole party to decide how the different colors
were blended. The thread seemed to be a tightly

twisted or "water-twisted" one, of fine wool—a thread which among our modern manufacturers, is considered of the greatest durability. Remembering the primitive modes possessed by the Indians, it is a marvel how they can produce such perfection. The women wear an outer garment falling from the neck to the ankle, girded at the waist, with tassels hanging from the girdle to the feet. Woolen leggins and high moccasins of different designs ornament their feet. The arms of the women are generally allowed to go bare, (except in such cooler days or parts of the year when they wear the wrapper or blanket spoken of above) exhibiting an arm and hand that many a so-called belle would be proud of, except that the hand will show the effects of a little closer intercourse with the material things of the world—dish-cloths and slop-pails—for instance. When they conceal those arms under the wrapper, however, it seems to be with as much grace as the best of 'em. Their hair is black and thick like the ordinary Indian, but they wear it with more taste, and something after the fashion of the Chinese women.

Their government is more after the civilized code than Indian. It consists of a governor; and what might correspond to our Lieut. Governor. An *Alcaldé* (or Mayor). Three *Tenientes* (or Police commissioners) who are responsible for the good behavior of the people, and twelve *Caziques* (or councilmen).

The head *Cazique* serves during life, and is called the *Wakamano*. The Governor also serves for life. The others are all elected yearly. The war chief during peace conducts the different kinds of hunts.

All orders—for the government and control of the tribes are given by the Governor in person from the top of the central house to his Caziques, and the orders are then distributed in the different locations or different sections of the grand house by them. They walk over the different places crying at the top of their voices, the order as given by the Governor— the story of the town cryers of old resuscitated.

In times of threatened raids from the Apachés or Navajoes, or impending dangers of war, they will not only congregate *en masse* in, and around their aerial city, but will drive up all their stock on the mesa, and once there they can bid defiance to an armed foe much greater in numbers than their own. It is supposed that these are the seven cities of Cibola which Coronado, with an armed force of Spaniards went, in 1540, from Mexico to conquer. It will be remembered how the inhabitants, although with primitive utensils of war, and with vastly inferior numbers, conquered the Spaniards. This was done by rolling huge boulders from the height, hurling missiles, arrows etc., at and down upon

their foes, as they would endeavor to ascend the mesa. "These people too, have their tradition of the flood. They say they have lived in these mountains and among these valleys ever since the world was destroyed by a great flood. Their ancestors got into a floating log which happened to be floating along. This log in the course of due time, and as the waters "soaked into the earth," landed on a high peak of the San Francisco Mountains. Shortly after their numbers increased rapidly, and the Apachés attacked them, killing the most of their tribe, and the remainder journeyed north to where they now live. Since this time, with their natural fortresses of defence, to be found in the mesa, together with their watchfulness, they have defended themselves against all odds. The old Governor—Governor Pino by name, can be often seen walking through his little city with the air and spirit of a truly modest guardian. On special or state occasions, the Governor carries a gold-headed cane which was given him by President Lincoln.

"In the centre of the town stand the remains of the old Catholic mission. It has not been used for worship for over one hundred years. How old the mission is, I am not possessed of suffiicient facts to say. Some records date back as far as 1732,—some older records being obliterated. Two old bells which remain still in the belfry are stamped 1689 and 1751.

THE ANTIQUITY OF THESE INDIANS—ARIZONA'S VICISSITUDES—
CONQUERED AT LAST—AMERICA'S DARK AGES—A COSTLY
BONFIRE—PRESCOTT — HUMBOLDT — BANCROFT — TO THE
LAND OF ANCIENT LORE BY RAIL !

———

IT is a well-known fact that the antiquity of these
people is one of the many subjects connected with
Arizona that is ; and has been ever since the time of
the Spanish conquest, taxing the investigation of man.
As Governor Safford once said : " There is probably
no portion of our domain where such a variety of
Indians live, speaking so many different dialects, as in
Arizona." And we might add of so many different
customs and natural characteristics. In regard to the
Zunis and Moquis it is now asked, " Are they Aztec,
Toltec, or what ? " The nearest we have got to it yet
is that they are " whatever " they may be. They
may be the descendants of the remnants of some par-
ticular tribe, or the remnants of a score of tribes
that suffered the incursions of the sixteenth century, consequent upon the invasion and conquest by
Cortez. What a revolution was there ! What a turn-

AN ANCIENT WAR DANCE OF THE APACHES.

ing upside down of institutions of a civilized, cultivated and refined people, who are now forgotten and
almost obliterated by the lapse of time. A people,
perhaps, scientific in the extreme, and whose institutions in many respects equalled, if not excelled, some
of those of our own civilization. With the opening
up of Arizona, the reward to us may be commensu-
rate with our difficulty and delay of getting a practical admission to her. More obstacles, and perhaps
oftener, have been thrown in the way to retard the
opening up of Arizona than perhaps any other portion of our country. In addition to the most formidable and desperate tribes of Indians that ever com-
bated the approach of civilization, the position of
Arizona, subjects us to the incursions of the treacherous Mexican banditti, who are as ready and willing to
profit by any misfortune or weakness of his neighbor
as the most ruthless Indian. Its position too, sub-
jected it to a great drawback in 1861 and '63 by our
civil war; and at a time when she was again budding
with success.

Some men, like communities are often found in
their egotism, congratulating themselves on the ad-
vance—the progression they are making, having an
infallible belief that progression, is a magnate taking
no back tracks, and meeting with no diversions ; that
we never lose, but always gain. That we did not lose

anything in the destruction of the Alexandrian library, or that if we did it was chaff compared to what we gained immediately after, or by the very destruction itself. Or that by the dark ages, although admit, ting they were irksome and disagreeable in themselves-nothing was lost. Others there are who claim to see a complete revolution in all things; who claim a comprehensive distinction between progress and change; who rather glory in finding that which was lost, claiming nothing new under the sun, and who concede that the dark ages are the great Machiavels of time who cunningly and stealthily crowd themselves in to baffle the philosopher in his course, and who simply cover up—hide, things for a limited period, for our employment and amusement in finding again.

From 1520 to 1530, then was the "dark age" of the North American Continent. Enough was covered up during those ten years to take all the science, work, and philosophy of centuries to unearth. This we know. But we do not know but that there is much that will never be discovered, nor even dreamed of. The most of these belong or are connected, in some way with the people of whom we have barely made mention, and of whom if volumes were written, which has already been done, one could scarcely do more. To what extent these facts exist may be made clearer by reference to the historian, Prescott. Prescott says: Book VI, Chap. 8:

"Yet the Aztecs must have been in possession of a much larger treasure, if it were only the wreck of that recovered from the Spaniards on the night of the memorable flight from Mexico. Some of the spoils may have been sent away from the capital; some spent in preparations for defence, and more of it buried in the earth, *or sunk in the waters of the lake.* Their menaces were not without meaning. They had, at least, the satisfaction of disappointing the avarice of their enemies.

"Cortez had no further occasion for the presence of his Indian allies. * * * * * * They carried off a liberal share of the spoils, of which they had plundered the dwellings—not of a kind to excite the cupidity of the Spaniards—and returned in triumph, (short-sighted triumph!) at the success of their expedition, and the downfall of the Aztec dynasty."

The memorable night alluded to above was that which is the present patron saint day of Mexico,—the day of St. Hypolito—and was selected and handed down as such from the circumstances connected with it.

Prescott also says, in speaking of the great quantities of the fine arts that is known to have existed among the Aztecs at the time of the Spanish conquest :—" The first archbishop of Mexico collected these paintings from every quarter, especially from Tezeuco, the most cultivated capital in Anahuac, and the great depository of the national archives. He then caused them to be piled up in a 'mountain heap,' as it is called by the Spanish writers themselves, in the market place of Tiateloco, and reduced them all to ashes."

Humboldt said :—" The Mexicans (Aztecs) were in possession of annals that went back to eight and a half centuries beyond the epoch of the arrival of Cortez in the country of Anahuac."

Bancroft tells us also, that the Aztecs retained many traditions and systems of the Toltecs " whose written annals they also preserved." He also says that at the time of the arrival of the Spaniards, there were great quantities of manuscript treasured up in the country.

A recent correspondence to the *Philadelphia Weekly Press*, says :—" At the time of the conquest of Mexico, Cortez found in Mexico a people millions in number, according to his account, enjoying a high order of civilization. Their government was a confederated empire of many states, a rather highly organized system, implying large political knowledge and practical statesmanship. Their religion was one of peace and love, if their temples filled with flowers and birds and fountains, and their daily life and conversation and

THE THREE INDIAN GIRLS:—AN-TI-NAINTS, PU-LU-SU
AND WI-CHUTS.

the many virtues transmitted to their descendants to-day—if these works are any evidence of their faith. They had wealth of gold and silver, and artistic workers in their precious metals. They had fine houses and great public works, temples, aqueducts, roadways. They had a calendar measuring the solar year more accurately than ours, and requiring readjustment not every four years, but only once in half a century. They had full records of their own civilization and history, but they were richer yet in the possession of ample and authentic records of the races before them."

All these annals and paintings met the same fate. All things in short connected with this people that fire would destroy, was obliterated from the face of the earth. It eclipsed the decline and fall of the Roman empire, and the worst features of history repeated themselves in the new world.

Science has heretofore been confined to the ancient recesses of the old world. But only a short space of time will elapse when the steam car alone will lead us to a new field of labor in this channel; curiosity and pleasure will follow closely in the wake of ambition's stronger impulse; and Arizona, New Mexico, and our southwest generally will resound with notes of the choicest ancient lore. The tide of pre-historic study, will be suddenly transferred to our very doors, and the flash of our ignited torch cast a lurid glare on even a pre-Adamite existence.

www.ingramcontent.com/pod-product-compliance
Lightning Source LLC
Chambersburg PA
CBHW032141080426
42733CB00008B/1159